Dear Daughter

Life Lessons from Your Mother

Written by Judy Smith

Photography by Lou Guarracino

Dear Daughter,

My strongest memory will always be the wonder of your precious infant hand holding on to my finger. It was at that moment when I became your protector and your guardian and you became my life. I know that I was put here for you and there is no measure for how much you are loved.

As you move through your journey know that you are beautiful, you are my shining light, my will, my angel. I will protect you with fierceness, support you with undying love, and help you achieve your goals with a vengeance.

I will always be your biggest cheerleader and will feel your pain, your heartache, your joys and your happiness as if they were my own. It is my joy to protect you and keep you from harm but I also want you to explore, learn, love, and experience it all. Spread your wings, take the world head on and be the incredible person you were meant to be.

I will always be here for you and you will forever be my baby.

With devotion,

Mom

Enjoy the Journey

Maintain a balance between getting to where you want to go and being happy as you get there. It's a great journey…enjoy all the detours along the way.

She's a Lady

There is a difference between a woman and a lady. There is a difference between a man and a gentleman. Always act like a lady and expect a man to be a gentleman.

Debt be Not

Avoid debt! This includes credit cards, student loans, personal loans and auto loans. This will help ensure your financial independence. Spend less than you earn, save as much as you can.

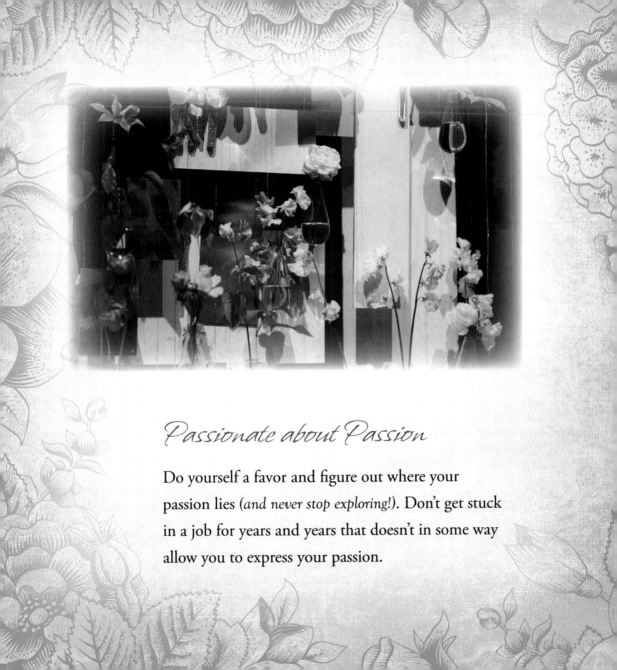

Passionate about Passion

Do yourself a favor and figure out where your passion lies *(and never stop exploring!)*. Don't get stuck in a job for years and years that doesn't in some way allow you to express your passion.

Mom, I'm in Love!

- Love can take you to new highs–and new lows.
- Sometimes the idea of love is better than love itself.
- The right man will view you with proper values and not as his property.
- If he makes you cry, he's not worth it. If he treats you like you are ordinary, he's not the right one.
- Fall in love when you are ready, not when you are lonely.
- Love is not perfect. It is full of good times, hard times and times when you simply want to give up.
- Sincere love is finding someone who will protect, respect, and appreciate you.

Venus and Mars

We truly are a different species from men. Accept and honor
the differences—*it will help you tremendously.*

Mr. Right

When you have found the right man *(I will help you make that decision!)*, be good to him and insist that he is good to you. Say "I love you" often and show it to him even more often. Think the best of him and speak the best of him to others.

Go With the Flow

Things won't always go as you had planned or hoped. In fact, this will happen often. Chances and events that seem to be unfortunate or undesirable may actually provide you with surprising results and advantages.

Wasted Emotions

Do not waste your precious time on jealousy and envy.

You Are Not Me and I Am Not You.

Let's try really hard to accept each other for our strengths and our weaknesses. No one else is exactly like you and no one else is exactly like me.

You need me as I am….and I need you just as you are.

When Life Makes You Cry...

- Eat ice cream.
- Take a nap.
- Buy a pair of shoes.
- Cry until your chest is empty of the painful feelings.
- Call me.

Spread Your Pretty Little Wings and Fly!

Rejoice in your individuality, no one else is exactly like you.

Flavors of Friends

Have friends of all backgrounds, ages and personalities. They will help you expand your interests and broaden your world.

Reading Rituals

Take a mini-vacation every day and spend time reading to enrich your life. When you find a book you particularly enjoy, be sure to share it with your friends or your mother.

Read everything you can about these amazing women:

- Susan B. Anthony
- Harriet Tubman
- Eleanor Roosevelt
- Billie Jean King
- Margaret Thatcher
- Clara Barton
- Marie Curie

Give Yourself a Stamp of Approval

You are your most important relationship. True happiness is when you feel good about yourself without feeling the need to have anyone else's approval. Once you have a healthy relationship with yourself, you can have a healthy one with others.

Food for Thought

Use your best china and silverware every day! Don't put them away for only special occasions. Every day is special, enjoy them whether you are dining alone or with friends and family. Preparing meals for others is a gesture of love.

> *Grow fresh herbs on your window sill.*
>
> *Add a pinch of cinnamon to your latte.*
>
> *Put your hands in the soil and grow some of your own food.*

Eat Your Vegetables!

Load up your shopping cart with these healthy power foods:

Greek Yogurt

Fat free organic milk

Salmon

Oatmeal

Flaxseed

Olive Oil

Avocado

Sweet Potatoes

Blueberries

Dark Chocolate

Pomegranate

Quinoa

Pumpkin

Lentils

Green Tea

Raspberries

Brown Rice

Lemons

Broccolli

Walnuts

Garlic

Should You Go or Should You Stay?

It's OK to leave me.
Travel the world if you
would like–just email or
call me regularly or send
me a postcard.

I didn't give birth to
burden you, I gave birth
to release you.

Live by the Light

Travel light, be light, live light.

Darkness fades by simply turning on the light.

Knowledge

Seek knowledge and
wisdom in all your life
experiences and the people
you meet, whether positive
or negative.

Wisdom is the key to a
powerful life of continual
growth and learning.

Be the You ...
You Were
Meant to Be

It is better to risk being
criticized for living true
to yourself than to be
loved for what you are
pretending to be.

The Gift of You

The best gift you have to give someone
is yourself. Your smile, your touch, your
time, your love are all timeless treasures.
Give them away often….but only to those
who deserve them.

Downward Facing Dog

Be it yoga, meditation, pilates or long walks…find
something that brings you peace and calms your mind.
Stay centered, stable and strong.

Butcher, Baker, Candlestick Maker

Choose your career wisely. Follow your passion and success will follow.

> Do you want to be your own boss or do you crave the stability of a steady paycheck?
>
> Interview your parents, relatives, mentors about their own personal career challenges.
>
> Clean up your social media presence! Your potential clients or boss may be watching!

Put Your Oxygen Mask on First

Love yourself first so that others can love you.

Care for yourself in every way.

Clean Your Room, Young Lady!

Demand order in your life and your surroundings. Having order invites calmness which precedes clear thought. When our mind is clear, we can make room for greater happiness and success. Clarity comes when there is order in the space where you exist.

Mom's Advice Column

- Family is the most important thing in life.
- Try a new food three times before you decide if you truly don't like it.
- Don't gossip. If you need to gossip, do so with me!
- Wrap presents so they look magical.
- Learn to sew.
- When wearing pantyhose somewhere, be sure to have an extra pair in your purse.
- Don't be a "mean" girl.

No tanning.

Always look for the toilet paper
before you close the door in a public restroom.

Designer handbags are worth it.

Write thank you notes—on personal stationary, preferably.
No thank you texts or emails.

It is not necessary to wash your hair every day.

Get your car oil changed frequently.

Never buy cheap mascara.

Visit museums.

Learn at least one other language.

Don't smoke. Don't even try it.

Get your sleep.

Never send an email or a message that you don't want the world to see.

I will always treat you like a little girl...deal with it.

Don't judge people by their relatives.

Talk slowly, but think quickly.

Wear sun screen!

Remove your makeup before going to bed.

Move on Over

When you accept a difficult situation this does not mean you are in agreement with it, only that you accept it and that you cannot change it. Your power lies in how you allow it to affect you.

Grab your inner power.

Be in the Moment

The moment is all there is. Let go of worrying about the future and focus on the moment.

Art of Forgiveness

You will be hurt, scorned, damaged and disappointed by the actions of others. You cannot control what others do, however you do have total control over how their actions affect you. Be sure to forgive yourself first, no one gets through life without making a few mistakes.

Grandma Has Been There and Done That

Get to know who your Grandmother is or was. She's had a lifetime of experience being a woman, so tap into her pearls of wisdom. Ask her about what it was like when she grew up, what she wanted to do. Ask for her advice.

Appreciate the Real You

Your happiness and self-worth are not
dependent on what others may think of you.
Always present the world with the real you,
the one you feel comfortable with.
Make the conscious decision to appreciate
yourself completely and enjoy being you.

Karma Is Real

Life experiences can be hard and they are supposed to be painful so we can absorb, heal, evolve and move forward. Never repeat mistakes. Everything has a cause and effect and comes full circle.

I Will Always Have Your Back

Surround yourself with people who love and support you.
Be sure to love and support them right back!

Back Off Fear!

Overcoming your fears is one of the most empowering things you can do for yourself. Prove to yourself that you can truly accomplish your goals.

Cut The Drama

Dramatic things will happen all on their own, choose to handle them with sensitivity and grace. Don't create unnecessary drama.

Take Time to Play

Never forget what it is like to be a child. Jump in puddles, skip with carefree laughter and embrace fun things in life, however seemingly frivolous they are. When the day to day activities become overwhelming, go into play mode and things will change as your stress level is reduced.

In The Still of Your Life

When thinking of everything, you feel nothing.
When thinking of nothing, you feel everything.

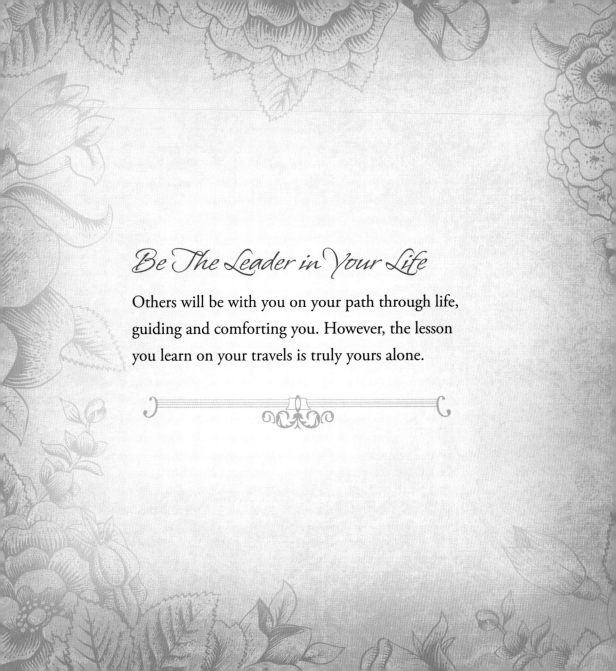

Be The Leader in Your Life

Others will be with you on your path through life, guiding and comforting you. However, the lesson you learn on your travels is truly yours alone.

No Comparison

Avoid comparing yourself to others.

This can lead you to overlook what is truly unique about you.

Celebrate You!

Bless You

Count your blessings, instead of your losses.
Take time everyday to reflect on three
things you are grateful for.
Say "thank you" to the people in your life
and do it often.

Change Your Attitude

Alter the way you view things and the things you view will change. Changing your attitude will always be the quickest route to changing your life.

Gracious Glasses

Choose to be a grateful person. Put on "gracious glasses" and look at the world with new eyes. Every day view things for which you are grateful. Even on the worst of days, when you look clearly, you will see blessings all around you.

Generosity

Give more to others than they expect and do so willingly.

Do not expect anything in return…it comes back to you.

Networking

Stay in touch with people you respect.

Welcome opportunities both personally and professionally.

Truth

Always be true to
yourself and you will
never feel the need to
be false to others.

Try Something New...
Often

Step out of your comfort zone and try something new.

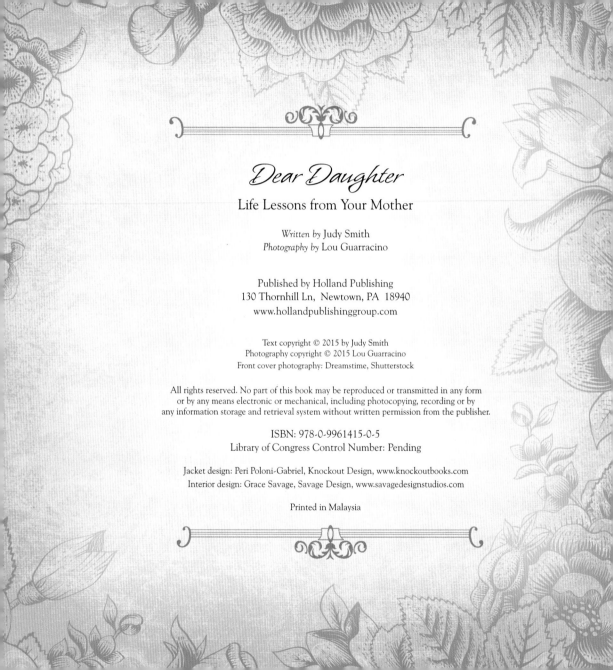

Dear Daughter

Life Lessons from Your Mother

Written by Judy Smith
Photography by Lou Guarracino

Published by Holland Publishing
130 Thornhill Ln, Newtown, PA 18940
www.hollandpublishinggroup.com

ISBN: 978-0-9961415-0-5
Library of Congress Control Number: Pending

Jacket design: Peri Poloni-Gabriel, Knockout Design, www.knockoutbooks.com
Interior design: Grace Savage, Savage Design, www.savagedesignstudios.com

Printed in Malaysia